Donald J. Trump's 7 Pillars of Strength for Triumph in Adversity

Jumel Pluviose

Donald J. Trump's 7 Pillars of Strength for Triumph in Adversity

The opinions expressed by the author are not necessarily those of Moon Shard Media.

5202 Corbridge Glen Ct., Katy Texas 77449 (254) 254 - 4712 | info@moonshardmedia.com

Moon Shard Media is committed to excellence in the publishing Industry.

Book Design copyright 2024 by Moon Shard Media. All rights Reserved.
Published in the United States of America
ISBN: 979-8-8692-4791-9
eISBN: 979-8-8692-4792-6

Disclaimer

This book, "Donald Trump's 7 Pillars of Strength for Triumph in Adversity," is a work of analysis and interpretation by the author based on publicly available information about Donald Trump. The author does not claim to have direct knowledge of Mr. Trump's thoughts, beliefs, or actions beyond what has been reported in the media, interviews, and other accessible sources.

While the author has made efforts to provide a comprehensive understanding of Mr. Trump s life, the content is subject to the limitations of available information, and certain aspects may be open to interpretation. Readers are encouraged to recognize that the perspectives presented in this book are shaped by the author's analysis and research rather than firsthand experiences or access to confidential information.

The purpose of this book is to explore the perceived pillars of strength that Mr. Trump may have exhibited in the face of adversity, as observed by the author through a thorough examination of publicly disclosed events. It is not intended to provide an exhaustive or definitive account of Mr. Trump's life, character, or beliefs.

Readers should approach the content critically and be aware that political figures can be complex and multifaceted. The author and publisher disclaim any responsibility for the accuracy or completeness of the information presented herein and advise readers to seek additional sources for a more comprehensive understanding of the subject matter.

This book is intended for informational and analytical purposes only and does not purport to offer personal or professional advice. The author encourages readers to form their own opinions and engage in further research to gain a well-rounded perspective on the subject.

TABLE OF CONTENTS

Acknowledgment

As the pages of "Triumph in Adversity: Donald Trump's 7 Pillars of Strength" come to life, I am compelled to express my gratitude to those whose support and contributions have shaped this narrative.

First and foremost, my appreciation extends to the individuals who have shared their insights, perspectives, and stories, contributing to the rich tapestry of this exploration. Your willingness to engage in meaningful conversations has added depth and authenticity to the pages that follow.

I am indebted to the tireless efforts of the editorial team whose commitment to clarity, coherence, and precision has been instrumental in bringing this work to fruition. Their dedication to refining ideas and crafting a compelling narrative has been invaluable.

To friends, family, and mentors who provided unwavering encouragement and a supportive environment during the creative process, thank you for your patience and belief in the project. Your presence has been a source of inspiration.

Finally, to the readers, I extend my heartfelt thanks. It is my sincere hope that this book resonates with you, sparks contemplation, and perhaps offers a fresh perspective on the qualities that define triumph in the face of adversity.

With gratitude,

Dedication

To my dearest friends and family,

You are the heartbeat of this journey. Your unwavering support, boundless love, and shared laughter have infused warmth into every word on these pages. In the tapestry of life, you are the vibrant threads that make each chapter rich and meaningful.

To my friends – the kindred spirits who have stood by my side through thick and thin – your camaraderie has been the compass guiding me through the twists and turns of creativity. Your belief in this project has been the wind beneath its wings.

To my family – the pillars of strength and the wellspring of my inspiration – your encouragement and understanding have been a constant source of fuel. This work is a testament to the values you instilled in me and the love that continues to shape my narrative.

And to you, dear reader – the one who embarks on this journey with an open heart and curious mind – thank you for allowing me to share these stories with you. May these pages bring you moments of reflection, inspiration, and connection.

With love and gratitude,

Preface

In the pages that follow, we embark on a riveting exploration of resilience, determination, adaptability, courage, perseverance, optimism, and the indispensable role of a robust support network — the seven pillars that underpin triumph in adversity. As we delve into the life of Donald J. Trump, a figure whose journey has ignited fervent discussions across the globe, we dissect the elements that shaped his path to success.

"Triumph in Adversity: Donald Trump's 7 Pillars of Strength" is not a political treatise; instead, it is an in-depth examination of the remarkable traits that propelled Trump through the highs and lows of his multifaceted career. Whether you find inspiration or skepticism in his story, this preface invites you to explore the core principles that defined his approach to challenges.

Each chapter scrutinizes one of the seven pillars, weaving together anecdotes, pivotal moments, and lessons gleaned from Trump's life. As we navigate through the narrative, we invite you to consider the universal relevance of these pillars — each a guiding light in the tumultuous journey of life.

This preface serves as an introduction to a narrative that transcends the political sphere, inviting readers to reflect on their own experiences, setbacks, and triumphs. In the end, "Triumph in Adversity" aims to inspire, provoke thought, and spark conversations about the nature of strength, resilience, and the enduring human spirit.

"Donald J. Trump's 7 Pillars of Strength for Triumph in Adversity"

Introduction

Triumph generally refers to a great victory or achievement, often accompanied by a sense of joy, pride, or satisfaction. It can be both a subjective and objective concept, depending on the perspective from which it is examined.

Subjective Viewpoint:

Triumph is highly subjective as well. It involves personal feelings of success, accomplishment, and fulfillment. Subjective triumphs can vary from person to person and may be tied to individual goals, values, or aspirations. For one person, overcoming fear may be a triumph, while for another, it might be completing a creative project.

Objective Viewpoint:

From an objective standpoint, triumph can be measured in concrete terms. For example, winning a championship, achieving a significant milestone, or accomplishing a difficult task can be considered objective triumphs. These are often quantifiable and observable achievements that are recognized by others.

Cultural and Societal Perspectives:

Triumph can also be viewed through cultural or societal lenses. What is considered a triumph in one culture may not hold the same significance in another. Societal norms and expectations can influence the perception of triumph, shaping the criteria by which individuals and communities measure success.

Temporal Viewpoint:

Triumph can be temporal, with short-term victories leading to long-term success. Conversely, what may appear as a triumph in the short term may not withstand the test of time. The context in which triumph is evaluated can impact its lasting significance.

Internal vs. External Triumphs:

Internal triumphs involve personal growth, self-discovery, or overcoming internal challenges. External triumphs, on the other hand, are often associated with tangible achievements visible to others. Balancing both internal and external triumphs can contribute to a more holistic sense of accomplishment.

Ethical Considerations:

Triumph may also be viewed through ethical lenses. Achieving success at the expense of others or through unethical means may be questioned even if it is objectively considered a triumph. The moral dimensions of triumph can add complexity to its definition.

In summary, triumph is a multifaceted concept with both subjective and objective dimensions. It is shaped by individual, cultural, societal, temporal, and ethical perspectives, making it a rich and nuanced concept in the human experience. In the end, the final personal perspective solidifies the ultimate essence of triumph.

What is the concept of adversity?

Adversity refers to challenging circumstances, situations, or events that individuals encounter in their lives. These challenges can come in various forms, such as personal setbacks, health issues, financial crises, or professional obstacles. Adversity is a universal part of the human experience, and how individuals respond to and navigate adversity can have a profound impact on both their personal and professional lives.

Impact on Personal Life:

Resilience Building: Adversity can serve as a crucible for personal growth and resilience. Facing and overcoming challenges can help individuals develop coping mechanisms, problem-solving skills, and emotional strength. It can lead to increased self-confidence and a sense of accomplishment.

Character Development: Adversity often tests a person's character and values. It can force individuals to reevaluate their priorities and make important life choices. For some, adversity can be a catalyst for personal transformation and the development of a stronger sense of purpose.

Emotional Toll: On the flip side, adversity can take an emotional toll, leading to stress, anxiety, depression, and other mental health challenges. Coping with adversity may require seeking support from friends, family, or mental health professionals.

Impact on Professional Life:

Adaptability: Adversity in the professional realm can come in the form of job loss, financial instability, workplace conflicts, or unexpected setbacks. Those who can adapt to changing circumstances and learn from adversity are often better equipped to succeed in their careers.

Career Growth: Overcoming professional challenges can lead to valuable learning experiences. For example, a failed project can provide insights that lead to future successes. Adversity can also inspire individuals to take risks, pursue new opportunities, and or re-strategize, or switch careers.

Leadership Skills: Leaders who have faced and conquered adversity are often more empathetic, adaptable, and effective in guiding their teams through tough times. Adversity can be a crucible that shapes exceptional leaders.

Networking and Support: Building a professional network and seeking support from mentors and colleagues can be crucial during times of adversity. These connections can provide guidance, opportunities, and a safety net when facing career challenges.

In essence, adversity is an inescapable facet of existence that exerts a profound influence on personal and professional growth. When confronted with adversity, individuals typically have two courses of action. One approach involves capitulating, evading, negating, or opposing adversity, while the alternative is to embrace it, acknowledging its inevitability and aligning oneself with its currents. Both avenues can chart a path, whether one of failure or success, in life's journey. An individual widely recognized for wholeheartedly embracing various forms of adversity is Donald J. Trump, the 45th President of the United States of America. Donald J. Trump's acceptance of adversity as an inextricable facet of his life has enabled him to cultivate resilience, adaptability, and the wisdom to seek support when necessary. Having honed these attributes from a young age, he has navigated a life continually marked by adversity, forging formidable strengths to navigate through any challenges. This book endeavors to scrutinize his approach to adversity, unveiling the seven pillars of strength essential for triumphing in the face of adversity.

Outlines

Strengthening one's capacity to overcome adversity often involves a blend of diverse attributes. In the case of Donald J. Trump, he appears to possess a comprehensive arsenal of these attributes, which have consistently played a crucial role in his history of enduring success. These attributes can be seen as the bedrock of his resilience when facing adversity. It's important to recognize that the prominence of these attributes can shift depending on specific circumstances and individual perspectives. I have identified seven key attributes that render Donald J. Trump an unstoppable force and arranged them in a sequence that illustrates their potential interplay and mutual reinforcement.

I firmly believe that these attributes are within the reach of every individual. The power lies in our hands to wield them, whether for virtuous or dubious pursuits.

Welcome to my second book: "Donald J Trump's 7 Pillars of Strength for Triumph in Adversity."

Chapter I

The duo Pillar 1 Resilience & Determination

The human spirit often reveals its remarkable capacity to overcome challenges and emerge stronger in the face of adversities of any nature. Resilience and determination stand out as two primary and inseparable pillars of strength that enable individuals to triumph over adversity. Although these qualities may seem distinct, they are closely intertwined, working in harmony to help individuals navigate through life's toughest moments. This combined chapter explores the profound connection between resilience and determination, illustrating how they complement each other and contribute to ultimate success when facing adversity. It will also demonstrate how and why Resilience and determination are the #1 & and 2 primary pillars of strength for Donald Trump for triumph in adversity.

According to AI (Artificial Intelligence), resilience is the ability to withstand, recover from, or adapt to challenging or adverse situations. It signifies mental and emotional toughness, the capacity to cope with stress, and the ability to bounce back from setbacks stronger than before. Resilience is the first attribute in this sequence. It's the foundation upon which the other attributes are built because, without resilience, it's challenging to persevere in the face of adversity.

Resilience helps individuals absorb shocks and maintain their equilibrium.

a. **Emotional Resilience:** This involves the capacity to manage emotions and maintain a positive outlook even in challenging circumstances. It enables individuals to process and cope with difficult feelings effectively.

b. **Social Resilience:** Building a strong support network of friends, family, and community can enhance resilience. The presence of a supportive community can provide emotional and practical assistance during adversity.

c. **Cognitive Resilience:** Developing problem-solving skills and a growth mindset can help individuals adapt to changing situations and find creative solutions to challenges.

Determination is the driving force, the unwavering commitment to achieving one's goals despite obstacles and setbacks. It is the fuel that propels individuals forward when faced with adversity. Determination encompasses:

A clear sense of purpose and well-defined goals provide a sense of direction during difficult times. Knowing what one is working towards keeps determination alive.

Determination is closely linked to persistence. It is the resolve to keep trying, even when the path is arduous, and success seems distant.

Individuals with determination are willing to put in the effort required to achieve their objectives.

Determination is not rigid. It requires the ability to stay focused on the end goal while remaining adaptable in the face of changing circumstances. This adaptability ensures that determination remains effective in various situations.

The Synergy of Resilience and Determination

Resilience and determination are two intertwined qualities that create a formidable and powerful fusion. Resilience serves as the shield that protects individuals from the negative impacts of adversity and provides the mental and emotional strength to persevere. Determination, in turn, harnesses the resilience-generated energy, directing it towards the achievement of goals. Together, they form a dynamic duo with profound effects:

Resilience acts as the armor, mitigating the adverse effects of setbacks, stress, and disappointments, enabling individuals to weather life's storms.

Determination acts as the driving force, channeling the inner strength gained from resilience towards progress, even in the face of the most daunting challenges.

The individuals who possess both resilience and determination are equipped not only to endure adversity but also to learn from it and ultimately triumph over it.

In life's journey, adversity is an inevitable companion. What sets individuals apart is how they respond to these challenges. Resilience and determination, while distinct qualities, are undeniably interconnected, serving as the bedrock of strength in adversity's shadow. The ability to rebound, adapt, and persist, coupled with an unwavering commitment to objectives, creates an indomitable force that empowers individuals to conquer even the most formidable obstacles. To attain success amidst adversity, one must nurture and cultivate both resilience and determination, for together, they form inseparable pillars of strength for triumph in adversity.

Resilience and determination stand as the primary pillars of strength and form an unbreakable foundation for personal growth and triumph in the face of adversity. Together, they forge a powerful synergy, enabling individuals to navigate life's challenges with grace and courage. Resilience, the ability to bounce back from setbacks, not only shields mental and physical well-being from the corrosive effects of stress and adversity but also sharpens problem-solving skills and fosters personal growth. Moreover, it paves the way for stronger interpersonal connections, as resilient individuals adeptly navigate conflicts and build lasting relationships.

Determination, the unwavering drive to achieve one's goals, complements resilience by providing the motivation and focus needed to persevere when obstacles loom large. In the crucible of adversity, determination transforms aspirations into tangible achievements, propelling individuals toward their objectives with relentless commitment. Moreover, determination fuels resourceful problem-solving, encouraging individuals to seek creative solutions and forge new paths in the face of challenges. This steadfast resolve contributes to psychological resilience, maintaining a positive attitude and a sense of control over circumstances, crucial for enduring emotional tolls.

The impact of this synergy extends beyond the individual; it inspires and motivates others who witness such strong determination in the face of adversity. The ripple effect of strength spreads, creating a culture of resilience and determination. Ultimately, this dynamic duo forms an investment in long-term success, helping individuals view adversity not as permanent failure, but as a temporary setback on the path to their goals. In essence, resilience and determination join forces, serving as beacons of hope and empowerment, illuminating the way forward even in the darkest of times. One well-known individual who has mastered this dynamic duo in its entire meaning is a former businessman and the 45th President of the United States of America, Donald J. Trump.

Donald Trump's Unyielding Resilience and Determination

From his formative years to seniority, Donald Trump exhibited an unshakable commitment and resolute determination to pursue his goals and convictions. Since childhood, he was known for his resolute nature and ambitious spirit. His refusal to conform to societal expectations and his unyielding pursuit of his interests, including early involvement in his family's real estate business, laid the foundation for his future success. These early experiences instilled in him the twin pillars of resilience and determination, forming the bedrock for his journey through life's trials and triumphs.

Donald Trump's early career as a real estate developer in New York City was marked by both adversity and triumph. In the 1980s, he confronted financial setbacks and challenging real estate market conditions. Yet, his refusal to capitulate and his determination to see his vision through resulted in the successful transformation of properties like the Commodore Hotel into the Grand Hyatt, emblematic of his business acumen and resilience. This early triumph set the stage for his subsequent accomplishments.

These experiences in the business world prepared him for the economic challenges he would face as President. His unwavering resilience in the face of economic downturns and his determination to rejuvenate the American economy became his guiding principles. His administration's initiatives in deregulation, tax cuts, and trade negotiations were hailed as triumphs amidst adversity, bolstering the stock market and job creation.

During his one-term tenure as President, Donald Trump encountered an unparalleled level of criticism, roadblocks, and challenges. However, his steadfast resistance in the face of intense political opposition transformed him into a formidable force. He consistently leaned on his dynamic duo of resilience and determination, often wearing down his adversaries and achieving victory. Throughout his tenure, he weathered relentless media criticism with remarkable resilience, allowing him to achieve significant policy victories such as criminal justice reform and international trade deals.

In the realm of international diplomacy, Trump faced significant criticism but remained undeterred in his ambitions. His determination to challenge traditional diplomatic norms led to victories like the renegotiation of international agreements, including the Iran nuclear deal, the Paris Agreement, and trade tariffs with Mexico and China. These were perceived as breakthroughs in overcoming entrenched obstacles. While opinions on these decisions varied, his unwavering commitment to reshaping U.S. foreign policy left an enduring mark on the international stage.

Donald Trump's resilience and determination to push forward with his policies, even in the face of formidable obstacles, ultimately led to triumphs. This steadfast commitment demonstrated how resilience and determination served as his primary source of strength when confronting dilemmas throughout his life. When unwavering determination and resilience yielded the desired outcomes, Trump's supporters hailed him as an unstoppable leader. This dynamic duo of traits inspired many to stand by him and support his agenda. Consequently, resilience and determination stand as the two primary pillars of strength that have fueled Donald Trump's triumphs in the face of adversity.

Chapter II

Pillar 2 - Determination

Determination is often considered the second pillar of strength in building the foundation for triumph in adversity due to its crucial role in propelling individuals forward when they face challenges. Here are several reasons why determination holds this pivotal position:

Sustained Motivation:

In summary, determination is the second pillar of strength because it plays a pivotal role in maintaining motivation, sustaining resilience, achieving goals, solving problems, nurturing psychological strength, inspiring others, and ensuring long-term success when facing adversity. It complements and amplifies the resilience established as the first pillar, making it a fundamental attribute on the path to triumph over life's challenges.

Certainly, here are four examples of how Donald Trump's determination has served as a pillar of strength for triumph in adversity, which also showcases his adaptability:

Business Turnarounds and Adaptability: Throughout his career in real estate and business, Donald Trump faced financial adversity on several occasions. His determination to overcome bankruptcy and financial setbacks in the 1990s was a testament to his resilience. Trump adapted to changing market conditions, diversified his business ventures, and ultimately triumphed by rebuilding his fortune. This adaptability, combined with his unwavering determination, allowed him to navigate turbulent financial waters successfully.

Political Resilience and Adaptation: During his presidency, Trump faced numerous political challenges and controversies. His determination to stay the course and pursue his policy agenda was evident. In the face of adversity, he adapted his approach by reshuffling his cabinet, engaging in diplomacy with world leaders, and signing bipartisan legislation such as criminal justice reform. This adaptability in the political arena allowed him to achieve significant policy victories.

COVID-19 Response and Swift Policy Adjustments: The COVID-19 pandemic presented an unprecedented global challenge during Trump's presidency. His determination to protect American citizens and the economy was unwavering. He adapted by implementing travel restrictions, mobilizing resources for vaccine development through Operation Warp Speed, and signing relief bills to support businesses and individuals affected by the pandemic. Trump's adaptability in responding to this crisis contributed to his administration's resilience in the face of adversity.

Trade Negotiations and Changing Tactics: In the realm of international trade, Trump's determination to address trade imbalances and protect American industries was a cornerstone of his presidency. He used tariffs and trade negotiations as tools to achieve his goals. When faced with resistance and challenges from trading partners, such as China, Trump adapted his tactics by engaging in both aggressive and conciliatory approaches. This adaptability allowed him to secure some trade agreements, demonstrating his determination to put American interests first.

In each of these examples, Donald Trump's determination served as a foundational pillar of strength that, when combined with his adaptability, allowed him to triumph over adversity and achieve his objectives in various aspects of his life and career.

Chapter III

Pillar 3 – Adaptability

Adaptability is the third pillar of strength in building the foundation for triumph in adversity because of its critical role in helping individuals navigate and thrive in ever-changing and challenging situations. Several reasons indicate why adaptability holds this pivotal position:

Adaptability fosters optimism and hope and helps reduce the stress associated with change and adversity. When individuals believe that they can adapt to changing circumstances, they maintain a positive outlook, which can be a powerful motivator during difficult times. This optimism fuels the determination to persevere. People who can adapt effectively tend to experience less anxiety because they have confidence in their ability to handle new challenges and situations.

Adversity often brings unexpected circumstances and uncertainties. Adaptability equips individuals with the skills to respond effectively to these unpredictable challenges. When a person can adjust their strategies and approaches swiftly, they are better prepared to face the unknown. Adaptability fosters flexible thinking, confidence, and problem-solving. When confronted with adversity, rigid thinking can be a hindrance. Those who can adapt are more likely to find innovative solutions and alternative routes to success, even when the initial plan falls apart. Adaptability complements resilience by enabling individuals to bounce back more efficiently. Resilience alone may help absorb shocks, but adaptability allows individuals to turn setbacks into opportunities for growth. It encourages a forward-looking perspective, where setbacks become stepping stones to success.

Adaptability cultivates versatility, which is valuable in diverse situations. Those who are adaptable can shift gears, change roles, and acquire new skills as needed, making them more versatile and valuable assets when facing adversity in various aspects of life.

Adaptable individuals are more in tune with the realities of their circumstances. They don't cling to unrealistic expectations or plans when those no longer apply. This alignment with reality enables them to make practical and effective choices.

Overall, adaptability equips individuals to respond effectively to unpredictable challenges, reduces stress, encourages flexible thinking and problem-solving, enhances resilience, cultivates optimism, builds on past experiences, and aligns individuals with the realities of their circumstances. When facing adversity, adaptability empowers individuals to not just survive but thrive in the face of change and uncertainty. Analyzing Donald Trump's way of adapting to past or current events, adaptability is classified as a pillar of strength allowing him to triumph in adversity. This has been demonstrated in various examples:

It is my impression that as a child, Donald Trump was remarkably different in personality as well as physically from his peers in all settings he could have been. He had a strong mind on his own and said unfiltered things that his peers and authoritative figures didn't want to hear. Few birds said that Donald Trump was quite chubby as a child. With all that, he must have been pushed back and been challenged or unaccepted by a few groups. Labeled his 'misbehavior' or not, Trump adapted himself to the environment. His subsequent successes in military academy and university that he did not give up on rejection or adversity, but adapted to challenges and triumphed in adversity.

His resilience and determination built on his adaptability which equips him with the confidence to respond effectively to unpredictable challenges, develop flexible thinking and problem-solving skills, and cultivate optimism in the business world. Throughout his career as a businessman, Donald Trump faced multiple business setbacks and bankruptcies. However, his adaptability shone through as he transformed these challenges into opportunities for growth. His ability to pivot and diversify his business ventures showcased his adaptability. This adaptability was then coupled with courage when he took bold risks, such as investing in high-profile real estate projects, demonstrating his willingness to face adversity head-on.

His past experiences in problem-solving and adaptability to confront unpredictable challenges empowered him to build enough confidence and optimism to dare to be a politician. Donald Trump displayed adaptability by transitioning from a business mogul to a political figure.

In the face of adversity, he successfully navigated the complex world of politics, adjusting his approach as needed to connect with voters and secure the Republican nomination. His courage was evident in his unapologetic stance on controversial issues, which solidified his appeal to certain segments of the population.

During his presidency, Donald Trump faced unprecedented challenges, including the COVID-19 pandemic. His adaptability was evident as he swiftly implemented economic policies to address the crisis, such as stimulus packages and deregulation to spur economic recovery. His courage was demonstrated by making tough decisions, such as banning travel from affected countries, to protect the nation's health and economy.

Foreign Policy: Trump's adaptability was on display in his approach to international relations. He engaged in unconventional diplomacy, using his business acumen to negotiate trade deals and international agreements. In the face of adversity, such as tense negotiations with North Korea, he remained resolute, showcasing his courage and willingness to confront difficult diplomatic challenges head-on.

In every instance explored, Donald Trump's remarkable adaptability emerged as a driving force, enabling him to navigate through challenges and emerge triumphant. His unwavering courage propelled him to take bold steps, solidifying his stature as a resilient and impactful figure in the realms of both business and politics. By deftly overcoming adversities, Trump showcased a unique ability to thrive in dynamic environments, leaving an indelible mark on the landscape of both business and presidential leadership.

Chapter IV

Pillar 4 - Courage

Courage is the fourth pillar of strength in building the foundation for triumph in adversity because it provides the essential inner fortitude required to confront fear, overcome obstacles, and persevere in the face of daunting challenges. Several key reasons support why courage is pivotal in this sequence:

Adversity often engenders fear and anxiety. Courage is the antidote to fear; it's the quality that allows individuals to confront their fears head-on. Whether it's the fear of failure, rejection, or the unknown, courage empowers individuals to act despite these fears. Courage is the catalyst for acting when outcomes are uncertain. Adversity is often accompanied by ambiguity and risks. Courageous individuals are willing to step into the unknown, make decisions, and take calculated risks even when the outcome is unclear. Courage enables individuals to tackle obstacles and setbacks with determination. When adversity presents formidable challenges, courage provides the inner strength needed to break through barriers and keep moving forward.

Resilience Booster: Courage, resilience, and determination go hand in hand. When people exhibit courage, it strengthens their resilience/determination by convincing them that they can overcome adversity. It reinforces the idea that setbacks are not insurmountable and that they can bounce back stronger.

Embracing Change: Many adversities involve significant changes in one's life. Courage allows individuals to embrace change with an open mind and heart. It encourages adaptability and the willingness to see change as an opportunity for growth.

Moral and Ethical Strength: Courage often involves standing up for one's principles and values, even when it's difficult or unpopular. In times of adversity, having the courage to uphold one's moral and ethical beliefs can be especially meaningful.

Leadership: Courage is a hallmark of effective leadership. Leaders who exhibit courage in the face of adversity inspire trust and confidence in their followers. They set an example for others to follow and provide guidance during challenging times.

Self-Discovery: Adversity can be a catalyst for self-discovery and personal growth. Courage allows individuals to explore their inner strengths and capabilities, uncover hidden potential, and emerge from adversity with a deeper understanding of themselves.

In essence, courage is the fourth pillar of strength because it provides the bravery and determination required to confront fear, take action in the face of uncertainty, overcome obstacles, boost resilience, inspire others, embrace change, uphold values, demonstrate leadership, and embark on a journey of self-discovery. It acts as a bridge between inner resolve and outward action, propelling individuals forward on their path to triumph over adversity.

Courage is essential for any kind of change one can imagine. The first and most important attribute needed for change is courage. Upon

Donald Trump's courage has served as a pillar of strength, enabling him to triumph in adversity and build upon the next pillar of positive optimism. Many people would agree with me that when it comes to being courageous, Donald Trump should hold the trophy in America in all American aspects had it been a competition or study, four he has accomplished so much only because of his courage. Which has been demonstrated in all his battlefields:

Despite Donald Trump's bold risks in business decisions, he has no fear of failure, rejection, or the unknown. He had never held a public office and had no formal or informal schooling for public office, still in 2016, his courage propelled him forward on the path to enter the American political race and defeat 17 republican candidates and later won the general election over a well-crafted lifetime political professional, Hilary Clinton. Which other American has dared to take such chances? By far, I only know Donald J Trump.

Donald Trump's courage has propelled him to openly come up with the 'American First Policy'. He was well aware of multiple difficulties that promoting that policy openly will engender nationally or internationally, among democrats or republicans. Still, his courage convinced him that he could handle any kind of dilemma arising from anywhere, level, or angle. In another way, Donald Trump had no fear of backfire or potential international retaliation. As controversial as he was, he had lots of criticism and resistance from national and international allies. Despite it all, he moved on with his agenda and was seen as a hero by many Americans, especially his supporters. In the end, Donald's trump courage in initiating American First policy had empowered him to triumph in adversity and set the tone for upcoming foreign policies.

Trump's courageous approach to international diplomacy enables him to tackle obstacles and setbacks with determination, which was evident in his negotiations with foreign leaders, including North Korea's Kim Jong-un. Despite the longstanding tensions between the two nations, Trump engaged in direct diplomacy, demonstrating his willingness to take bold steps for peace. This courage not only contributed to easing tensions but also fostered positive optimism about the potential for improved international relations. Credit should be given to him for boldly trying despite high levels of tensions with prior administrations.

During his presidency, Trump enacted bold economic policies, such as tax cuts and deregulation, aimed at stimulating economic growth. His courage in implementing these policies, despite opposition, resulted in a strong pre-pandemic economy with record-low unemployment rates. This economic success fueled positive optimism among Americans about their financial prospects and the country's economic future. He triumphed over high levels of resistance to pass those policies.

Trump's administration took courageous steps toward criminal justice reform, passing the First Step Act. This bipartisan legislation aimed to address issues of mass incarceration and provide opportunities for rehabilitation. By signing this bill into law, Trump demonstrated the courage to tackle a complex and deeply entrenched issue, fostering optimism for a fairer and more just criminal justice system. His courage enables him to try and do what other administrations had dared to try or do.

Whether one agreed or disagreed with the outcome, Trump's administration brokered historic peace agreements between Israel and several Arab nations, known as the Abraham Accords. These breakthroughs were the result of courageous diplomacy and a willingness to challenge traditional approaches to Middle East peace. The signing of these accords instilled positive optimism about the prospects for stability and cooperation in the region.

In each of the above-mentioned instances, Donald Trump's courage emerged as a powerful pillar of strength, enabling him to triumph in the face of adversity. His unshakable determination and fearlessness were instrumental in steering various aspects of his leadership toward transformative change and progress.

In essence, the presence of courage in leadership can serve as a beacon of hope in times of adversity. Donald Trump's demonstration of courage not only allowed him to overcome formidable challenges but also kindled optimism for the potential for positive change and progress in these critical areas. It underscores the idea that in the face of adversity, courage can be a driving force for transformation and advancement on both national and international fronts.

Chapter V

Pillar 5 - Perseverance

Perseverance, often referred to as tenacity, is the fifth pillar of strength in building the foundation for triumph in adversity. It plays a crucial role in helping individuals overcome challenges and achieve their goals despite obstacles and setbacks. Here's why perseverance is a fundamental attribute in this sequence:

1. Perseverance is the quality that enables individuals to maintain consistent effort over an extended period. When facing adversity, it's common to encounter roadblocks and discouragement. Perseverance ensures that individuals keep working towards their objectives, even when progress is slow or difficult.

2. Perseverance is the willingness to stay committed to a course of action, no matter how challenging it becomes. This steadfastness is what sets apart those who succeed in the face of adversity from those who give up.

3. Perseverance allows individuals to view failure as a learning opportunity rather than a defeat. Each failure becomes a stepping stone toward success. Perseverance often leads to personal growth and self-discovery. The process of pushing through adversity, learning from failures, and achieving goals can result in increased self-confidence, resilience, and a deeper understanding of one's capabilities. It doesn't mean blindly

sticking to a single approach. It involves adaptive persistence, which means being open to adjusting strategies and tactics while maintaining the overall commitment to the goal. This flexibility is crucial for triumph in adversity.

4. Perseverance enhances resilience by reinforcing the belief that one can overcome adversity. When people persevere through difficult times, it strengthens their resilience, making them more capable of withstanding future challenges. In my first book 'Donald Trump, The Innovative Genius! Carving an Indelible Legacy', the concept of TRP (Tenacity, Resilience, and Perseverance) was introduced as a winning mindset. Please check it out for further understanding.

5. Perseverance is what turns aspirations into achievements. It ensures that individuals not only set ambitious goals but also work relentlessly to attain them. In the face of adversity, it's often the sheer determination to persevere that carries individuals through. Adversity can sometimes lead to plateaus or periods of slow progress. Perseverance is the driving force that propels individuals through these plateaus, helping them break through to the next level of success.

Mr. Trump is well-recognized for his tenacity, resilience, and unwavering perseverance in both his private and public life. This innate trait of his is a defining aspect of his personality, especially as a businessman and leader.

All along, Donald Trump has consistently exhibited perseverance as a pillar of strength. Here are a few examples showcasing his determination in the face of adversity, spanning his childhood, business ventures, and his presidency:

Childhood:

Trump's childhood was marked by a strict and demanding father, Fred Trump. In the effort to meet high expectations and pressure to succeed imposed by his dad, Donald Trump had no choice but to persevere regardless of the situation presented. Hence, at an early age, perseverance became a part of him; he cultivated it and incorporated it into his life as a strong work ethic. He excelled in school and developed resilience, which later contributed to his success in business and politics.

Business:

Trump faced numerous business setbacks and financial challenges throughout his career. During those setbacks, most people would have let it go and say it wasn't meant to be, others could have disregarded the root cause of the problems and left it to the good nature. Donald Trump isn't for any of that. Donald Trump's fifth pillar strength of perseverance built him up to shape his destiny. As so, regardless of the situation, he must persevere to pull out his triumph out of the adversity presented. In the 1990s, his real estate empire teetered on the brink of bankruptcy, but he persevered by negotiating deals with creditors and bouncing back financially.

He had 6 famous bankruptcies which were unprecedented. Many people believed that his era would come to an end; instead, he played his chest brightly so that he managed to rebuild his business empire and became a successful real estate developer, hotelier, and TV personality. Donald Trump plays to win and whatever (time, resources, and intelligence) it takes to triumph in adversity, his pillar of resilient and perseverant work ethic gets stronger and more reliable. His strength to persevere in the face of challenges showcased his steadfast commitment to success.

To differentiate the first campaign from the second unprecedented former or ex-president running for office, I classified those two occasions as: Outsiders and former / ex-president candidates.

Outsider campaign:

Primary Election Battles

Donald Trump's entry into the Republican primary was met with skepticism and opposition from within his party. As a political outsider, he faced well-established candidates and party elites. Despite the odds, Trump persevered through a series of state primaries, gradually gaining momentum and confidence, and winning over voters with his unconventional and unprecedented style. His resilience in the face of doubt and rivalry within the GOP ultimately led to him securing the party's nomination.

In October 2016, just weeks before the presidential election, a damaging video surfaced in which Trump made controversial remarks. The incident created a significant political storm, with many questioning his candidacy. Instead of succumbing to the pressure, Trump displayed resilience by acknowledging the controversy, classifying it as locker talk, and refocusing his campaign message. Despite widespread predictions of a campaign collapse, he persevered and weathered the storm to continue campaigning vigorously and strategically.

In the final weeks leading up to the election, Trump faced a barrage of negative media coverage and intense scrutiny. Accusations (to add supporting evidence) and controversies led to predictions of an imminent defeat surrounding his campaign. Undeterred, Trump persevered to maintain a relentless campaign schedule, holding multiple rallies per day in key battleground states. His ability to persevere through the intense scrutiny and keep a strong public presence showcased a remarkable level of resilience. Despite being an outsider, damaging video, negative media coverage, accusations, and controversies, Donald Trump persevered until Election Day to win several crucial swing states and ultimately secure victory over a lifetime political wizard, Hilary Clinton.

Presidency:

In the period following his presidency, former presidential candidate Donald Trump has encountered numerous challenges from various fronts, and it appears that these challenges are far from resolution. Being Donald J Trump and showcasing an exceptional dramatic campaign to win the presidency of The United States of America, only a fool would expect a drastic behavioral or situational change from candidacy to the presidency. Donald Trump left nothing behind, especially, his armory and strength to approach any battle as a well-trained warrior. As so during his presidency, Trump faced significant political adversity and criticism from various quarters. He continued to push forward with his agenda, tackling issues like tax reform, deregulation, and criminal justice reform, demonstrating his resilience in the face of opposition.

The negotiation and eventual signing of the Abraham Accords in 2020, which led to the normalization of relations between Israel and several Arab nations, showcased his perseverance in pursuing peace and diplomacy in the Middle East, despite longstanding conflicts.

He also displayed perseverance in trade negotiations, particularly with China. Despite ongoing tensions and trade disputes, he continued to engage in negotiations and aimed to secure better deals on behalf of the United States.

Trump's response to the COVID-19 pandemic demonstrated his determination to expedite vaccine development through Operation

Warp Speed. His administration's efforts to accelerate the vaccine development process showcased a commitment to addressing a global crisis.

Throughout his presidency, Trump faced numerous investigations and political controversies, more than enough for a major depression. Despite these obstacles, he continued to pursue his policy goals, including tax reform and deregulation, displaying his determination to see his agenda through to completion.

While opinions about Donald Trump's actions and decisions vary widely, there is no doubt that he has displayed perseverance in the face of adversity throughout his life, whether in business, politics, or personal challenges.

In summary, perseverance is the fifth pillar of strength because it empowers individuals to sustain effort, demonstrate grit, learn from failure, enhance resilience, achieve their goals, overcome plateaus, practice adaptive persistence, inspire others, and experience personal growth. It is the unwavering commitment to continue striving for success, even in the face of the most challenging adversity, that makes perseverance an indispensable attribute on the path to triumph.

Chapter VI

Pillar 6 – Optimism

Optimism is the sixth pillar of strength in building the foundation for triumph in adversity. It is a fundamental attribute because it shapes one's mental and emotional approach to challenges, allowing individuals to maintain hope, resilience, and a constructive perspective when facing adversity. The following examples explain why and how optimism plays a crucial role in this sequence:

Optimism is characterized by a positive mindset. It enables individuals to maintain a hopeful and constructive outlook even in the face of adversity. This mindset sets the stage for finding opportunities within challenges. Optimism reinforces resilience by helping individuals bounce back from setbacks more effectively. Optimistic individuals are more likely to view adversity as a temporary distraction (setback) rather than a permanent defeat, which aids in faster recovery.

Optimism is linked to improved emotional well-being. It helps individuals manage stress, anxiety, and depression better, which are common emotional responses to adversity. Optimistic individuals tend to experience less emotional distress during difficult times, which leads to better decision-making and problem-solving skills. When people believe that challenges can be overcome, they are more motivated to seek solutions and take proactive steps to address difficulties. Individuals with an optimistic perspective tend to make decisions with a focus on potential positive outcomes, which can lead to more advantageous choices. Optimism contributes to long-term resilience. Individuals who maintain a positive outlook, are more likely to build the habits and skills necessary to weather future adversities successfully.

In summary, optimism nurtures a positive mindset, reinforces resilience, promotes emotional well-being, fosters problem-solving, motivates and determines action, encourages adaptive thinking, connects the dots, contributes to long-term resilience, and enhances decision-making and problem-solving skills. It is the optimistic belief that adversity can be overcome and that better days lie ahead that empowers individuals to maintain their strength and determination throughout challenging times, ultimately leading to triumph over adversity.

Whether agree or disagree, Donald Trump's optimism has been one of his pillars of strength enabling him to triumph in adversity which also builds upon the next pillar of supportive and resilient networks. Here is how optimism has been manifested in Donald Trump's life:

While I can provide information on instances where Donald Trump has used optimism in his career, it's important to note that opinions on his approach and the impact of his optimism can vary. Additionally, the concept of "triumph in adversities" is subjective, and interpretations may differ. Here are examples from Trump's childhood, business, and political career where optimism played a crucial role:

Donald Trump has often spoken about the positive influence of his father, Fred Trump who, I believe, was the first and primary influencer in Donald Trump's life as a child and young adult. The optimism instilled in him during his formative years likely contributed to his later ventures and successes. I also do not doubt that Donald Trump potentiated his optimistic personality trait tremendously at the military academic school. I imagined every achieved goal or successful completion of a milestone boosted Trump to set bigger and more complex ones in the military academy. I truly can't measure the level or stage at which Donald Trump's optimism was when graduated from military academy school, but combining his father's contribution to the school, I am compelled to believe that he was very, very optimistic.

Business:

As he ventured into the real estate business field, Trump faced multiple challenges in the real estate market during economic downturns. However, his optimism and confidence in the market's eventual recovery led him to master the art of perseverance.

He often spoke about viewing setbacks as opportunities for future success (reference please). As such, he faced financial difficulties in the early 1990s, he remained optimistic with a positive outlook and created strategies to navigate the bankruptcies with all its intricacies. His optimism has fostered his ability to turn things around and successfully restructure his debts, preserving the Trump Organization. In my opinion, that is a great example of turning something negative into positive with the strength of being optimistic.

His optimism was evident in his role as the host of "The Apprentice." His catchphrase, "You're fired," was paired with a belief in the contestants' potential for success, emphasizing the importance of perseverance and determination. Applying his catchphrase "you're fired" without hesitation or fear of resistance indicates his optimism and belief in establishing a clear tone, a characteristic that resonates with his leadership style, where he expects others to fall in line. Throughout his presidential campaign, Trump projected an optimistic vision for America. His slogan, "Make America Great Again," conveyed a sense of optimism about the country's future and a belief in its potential for greatness.

Trump's administration often highlighted positive economic indicators and growth. He expressed optimism about the impact of tax cuts and deregulation on the economy, aiming to spur job creation and business expansion. Amid economic downturns and uncertainties, Trump's positive optimism was evident in his messages of economic revival. His unwavering belief in the resilience of the American economy encouraged business leaders and investors to remain optimistic about the future. This optimism fostered supportive networks among businesses and government agencies, leading to coordinated efforts to stimulate economic growth.

In diplomatic negotiations, Trump often took an optimistic approach, expressing confidence in his ability to make deals. For example, he pursued dialogue with North Korea, expressing optimism about the potential for denuclearization on the Korean Peninsula.

It's essential to recognize that perceptions of Trump's optimism may differ, and these examples highlight instances where he publicly demonstrated a positive outlook in various aspects of his life and career. In each of these examples, Donald Trump's positive optimism not only helped him triumph in the face of adversity but also fostered supportive and resilient networks of individuals, organizations, and government entities who shared his vision and worked together to achieve common goals in various critical areas. Optimism by far has been classified as Donald Trump's sixth pillar of strength for triumph in adversity. That pillar helps him to amass numerous individuals, institutions, and groups as supporters on which he builds resilient networks.

Chapter VII

Pillar 7 - Support and Resilient Networks

The seventh pillar of strength in building the foundation for triumph in adversity is having a supportive and resilient network. While it may not be an individual attribute like resilience, determination, or optimism, the presence of a strong support network is crucial because it provides a critical external resource that can significantly bolster one's ability to overcome adversity. Here's why having a supportive and resilient network is a pivotal component:

A supportive network, whether it consists of family or friends, groups or institutions, colleagues or mentors, offers emotional and moral support during challenging times. Knowing that there are people who care about your well-being and are there to listen, empathize, and encourage can be immensely comforting and motivating. Trusted individuals within your network can offer valuable perspectives and advice. When facing adversity, it's common to become emotionally invested or to have tunnel vision. A network can provide alternative viewpoints and suggest solutions that might not have been apparent otherwise.

A resilient network serves as a safety net, can be a source of tangible resources, reinforces your resilience often includes individuals who have faced adversity themselves. Their shared experiences can be a source of inspiration and guidance. They can offer practical insights and share how they overcame similar challenges.

Networks can be a source of tangible resources. Whether it's financial support, access to information, job referrals, or other forms of assistance, having a supportive network can provide resources that help mitigate the impact of adversity.

A network can help keep you motivated and accountable. Knowing that others believe in your ability to overcome adversity can inspire you to keep going. Additionally, sharing your goals and progress with others can create a sense of accountability that encourages you to persevere.

Networks often include individuals with diverse backgrounds, skills, and perspectives. This diversity can be invaluable when problem-solving or seeking creative solutions to adversity. Different viewpoints can lead to innovative approaches.

A resilient network reinforces your resilience. Interacting with individuals who have overcome their challenges can instill confidence and strengthen your belief that you can bounce back from adversity as well.

Adversity can be isolating, and feelings of loneliness can exacerbate its emotional toll. A supportive network reduces this isolation by providing a sense of belonging and connection, which can improve mental and emotional well-being. A supportive network can help reduce stress. Stress reduction is particularly crucial during adversity when high-stress levels can negatively impact decision-making and overall health.

Building a resilient network serves as a safety net. In case of severe setbacks or unforeseen challenges, having a network that can offer assistance and support can prevent a crisis from becoming unmanageable.

In conclusion, a supportive and resilient network is the seventh pillar of strength because it provides emotional support, diverse perspectives, shared experiences, resources, motivation, and accountability. It reduces isolation, helps build resilience, reduces stress, and serves as a safety net during adversity. It is the combined strength and collective wisdom of a network that can make a significant difference in an individual's ability to triumph over adversity.

Donald Trump's supportive and resilient networks

Donald Trump's ability to build supportive and resilient networks has been a pillar of strength, enabling him to triumph in adversity and navigate challenges effectively. Here are four examples illustrating this:

While Donald Trump's life and career have been marked by various challenges and controversies, it's important to note that perspectives on his use of a supportive and resilient network may vary. Here are some instances where he has relied on networks in different aspects of his life:

Donald Trump within the nuclear family supports

The nuclear family refers to a family unit consisting of two parents and their children living together in a single household. "Nuclear family support" typically refers to the emotional, financial, and practical assistance that members of this core family unit provide to each other. This support can encompass various aspects of daily life, including caregiving, financial contributions, and emotional well-being. I believe that growing up Donald Trump received all those various aspects of nuclear support a child is supposed to have. I must acknowledge that each nuclear family's support varies depending on multiple factors of politico-social aspects of the country in which the person lives, the financial and social status of the family, and more importantly cultural and belief system. I can't even think of a child who is not loved by a few family members. As such, Trump hasn't only had nuclear family support but also extended family support.

Nuclear and extended family support/network played a crucial role in shaping the overall well-being and functioning of Donald Trump, as he relied on them for various forms of support in his day-to-day life growing up.

The foundation of a supportive and resilient network must be built upon one's own family. It often starts with the nuclear family, extended family members, and community. Donald Trump is a prime example of this credo whose father, Fred Trump was the primary network mentor who started to shape his business acumen. His father provided financial support and guidance, helping him establish a foundation for his future endeavors.

Trump attended the New York Military Academy, where he received structure and discipline. The University of …. Where he learned ….

The connections he made during his school years and the mentorship he received could be considered part of his early network.

Early in his career in the real estate industry, Trump built a solid and resilient network. His connections with influential figures in New York real estate played a crucial role in his ability to secure deals and navigate the complexities of the industry.

Donald Trump's connections with the most prominent and influential figures in New York real estate included various individuals who played significant roles in the industry. Some key figures in Trump's real estate network included:

Fred Trump (Father): Donald Trump's father, Fred Trump, was a successful real estate developer in his own right. He provided support, guidance, and financial backing to his son, helping him enter the real estate business.

Roy Cohn, a prominent attorney known for his aggressive and controversial tactics, was a mentor and close associate of Trump. Cohn provided legal counsel and representation for Trump in various real estate dealings.

George Ross was an executive vice president and senior counsel in the Trump Organization. He played a key role in Trump's real estate ventures and was a trusted advisor in negotiations and deal-making.

Barbara Res served as an executive vice president of the Trump Organization and played a significant role in the construction of Trump Tower. Her contributions to major projects were part of Trump's success in the real estate sector.

The LeFrak family, prominent real estate developers in New York, had connections with Trump. Richard LeFrak and Donald Trump collaborated on certain real estate projects, contributing to each other's successes.

While primarily known as an investor rather than a real estate figure, Carl Icahn had interactions with Trump and was involved in some of Trump's Atlantic City casino ventures. Icahn's financial support and involvement contributed to Trump's business dealings.

The Tishman family, with figures like Robert Tishman, were influential in the New York real estate scene. Trump had connections with them through various real estate transactions and partnerships.

These connections, among others, helped Donald Trump navigate the complex world of New York real estate and establish himself as a prominent figure in the industry. It's important to note that the nature of these relationships varied, and not all interactions were uniformly positive or without controversy.

Legal and Financial Advisors:

Throughout his extensive business career, Donald Trump strategically assembled a robust team of lawyers, accountants, and financial advisors to adeptly navigate the complex landscape of corporate dealings and legal challenges. At the core of this team was his lawyer, a trusted confidant who played a pivotal role in handling a spectrum of legal matters, offering immediate guidance, and ensuring attorney-client privilege for confidential discussions.

Complementing his lawyer, Trump maintained a broader network of legal and financial professionals. This multifaceted team addressed challenges ranging from lawsuits to regulatory compliance, ensuring his business ventures adhered to legal norms. Financial advisors and accountants played a crucial role in optimizing deals, managing tax implications, and mitigating risks.

This comprehensive team approach showcased Trump's proactive stance in anticipating and addressing challenges. The intricate interplay between legal, financial, and advisory professionals allowed him to navigate the complexities of the business world effectively, presenting a united front against legal challenges and strategically positioning himself in negotiations. Notably, figures like Michael Cohen, 'The Fixer' and Rudy Giuliani, serving as his attorney, brought high-profile attention to the dynamics of Trump's legal team during business dealings and his presidency.

Brand and Media Relationships:

Trump's success in the entertainment industry and his reality TV show, "The Apprentice," expanded his network into the realms of media and branding. This network proved valuable during his presidential campaign, as he leveraged his celebrity status and media relationships.

Donald Trump's triumphs in the entertainment industry, particularly through his reality TV show "The Apprentice," not only elevated his celebrity status but also broadened his network into the influential realms of media and branding. This strategic expansion played a crucial role during his presidential campaign, where Trump capitalized on his established connections to gather more supporters and build a robust political network.

The symbiotic relationship between Trump, the media, and branding became a potent force. His celebrity status, cultivated through years in the spotlight, allowed him to command attention and shape narratives. The media, in turn, was drawn to the sensationalism and controversy that often surrounded him, providing Trump with a platform to amplify his messages and engage with the public on a massive scale.

Additionally, Trump's expertise in branding became a linchpin in his political strategy. His ability to craft a distinctive and memorable image, coupled with his media-savvy approach, helped him resonate with a broad audience. The familiarity and recognition built through his branding efforts contributed significantly to the formation of a dedicated support base.

Furthermore, the pre-existing network of business relationships, legal advisors, and financial experts that Trump had cultivated throughout his career seamlessly merged with his media and branding connections.

This convergence created a formidable coalition, reinforcing his political aspirations with a diverse and influential support system.

In essence, Trump's success in the entertainment industry laid the foundation for a powerful network that seamlessly translated into the political arena. His adept use of media, celebrity status, and branding not only garnered him more supporters but also solidified a strong network that played a pivotal role in his political journey. The intersection of these elements showcased the interconnected nature of Trump's multifaceted approach, where entertainment, media, branding, and politics converged to shape his trajectory in the public eye.

Politics:

Donald Trump's triumph in adversity can be attributed to the robust and multifaceted network he meticulously built throughout his political career. This network served as a pillar of strength, providing crucial support at various levels.

Influential Republican Backing:

One of the cornerstones of Trump's success was his ability to garner the support of influential Republicans and political figures. This backing was particularly evident during his presidential campaign, where key figures within the Republican Party openly endorsed him. By aligning with established political leaders, Trump demonstrated a strong and strategic political network. This network not only provided him with credibility but also served as a source of guidance and expertise.

Grassroots Movement:

Trump's connection with his voter base, often referred to as his grassroots movement, was instrumental in his journey to the presidency. Through effective use of social media and energetic rallies, he cultivated a dedicated and vocal network of supporters. This grassroots support not only bolstered his campaign but also created a solid foundation of loyalty among a significant segment of the population. This network proved resilient in the face of adversity, weathering challenges and contributing significantly to his political triumphs.

Cabinet and Administration Diversity:

Upon assuming the presidency, Trump extended his network to his cabinet and administration. Instead of surrounding himself with like-minded individuals, he appointed advisors with diverse backgrounds and perspectives. This diverse network played a crucial role in shaping policy decisions and navigating complex issues. By drawing on a wide range of expertise, Trump demonstrated resilience in the face of adversity, showcasing an ability to adapt and make informed choices.

It's important to note that opinions on the nature and impact of Trump's network may vary. While some see it as a strength, others may critique certain associations. Nonetheless, the undeniable fact remains that Trump's ability to build and leverage a supportive network at various levels played a vital role in his ability to triumph over adversity in the realm of American politics.

Donald Trump's Network of Supportive Administration

1. Judicial Appointments: During his presidency, Trump worked closely with conservative organizations and legal experts to build a strong network of support for his judicial appointments. This network helped him successfully nominate and confirm a record number of federal judges, including three Supreme Court justices. These appointments had a lasting impact on the judiciary, shaping the direction of legal decisions for years to come and solidifying his influence on the legal system.

2. Trade Negotiations: In his efforts to renegotiate trade agreements, such as the United States-Mexico-Canada Agreement (USMCA) and the Phase One trade deal with China, Trump relied on a network of trade advisors, economists, and industry leaders. This collaborative network played a crucial role in achieving trade deals that aligned with his administration's goals, mitigating potential economic challenges, and advancing his "America First" agenda.

3. COVID-19 Vaccine Development: The Trump administration's Operation Warp Speed initiative brought together pharmaceutical companies, government agencies, and research institutions to accelerate the development of COVID-19 vaccines. This resilient network of experts and stakeholders worked tirelessly to expedite vaccine research, testing, and distribution. Trump's leadership in forming and supporting this network contributed to the rapid development and distribution of multiple vaccines, a key milestone in the fight against the pandemic.

4. Criminal Justice Reform: Trump's efforts to pass criminal justice reform, including the First Step Act, involved building a diverse coalition of supporters from both political parties, civil rights organizations, and law enforcement agencies. By fostering this supportive network, he overcame political challenges and resistance to enact meaningful criminal justice reform, addressing issues such as sentencing disparities and prison reform.

In these examples, Donald Trump's ability to establish and leverage supportive and resilient networks played a central role in his ability to triumph over adversity and achieve his policy objectives, whether in the areas of judicial appointments, trade negotiations, public health, or criminal justice reform. These networks helped him navigate challenges and advance his policy agenda effectively.

Trump's success in building and utilizing supportive networks can be seen as a consistent theme throughout his life, from his early years in real estate to his entertainment career and ultimately in the political arena.

Donald Trump's journey to success has been fortified by a robust network, beginning with the foundational support of his family, particularly his father Fred Trump, which paved the way for his entry into the real estate realm. As he delved into the intricacies of New York real estate, Trump strategically surrounded himself with influential figures, forging a resilient network that provided invaluable guidance, legal counsel, and financial backing.

Expanding his horizons into the entertainment industry, Trump's network evolved to encompass media and branding relationships. Crafted through years of experience and triumphs in the public eye, this network became a formidable asset during his groundbreaking presidential campaign. The synergy between entertainment, media, branding, and politics demonstrated the multifaceted nature of his strategic approach.

In the realm of politics, Trump's prowess in garnering support from influential Republicans, cultivating grassroots movements, and diversifying his cabinet underscored the strength of his political network. This network played an important role in his victories, spanning the presidential campaign and translating into successful policy initiatives such as judicial appointments, trade negotiations, COVID-19 vaccine development, and criminal justice reform.

While opinions on Trump's network may differ, its undeniable impact is evident. His adept utilization of supportive and resilient networks served as pillars of strength, enabling him to surmount adversity, make informed decisions, and ultimately achieve success across diverse fields. The diverse perspectives, resources, and expertise offered by these networks formed an integral part of Trump's ability to navigate challenges and triumph over adversity.

Conclusion

Donald Trump's remarkable career, marked by success in both business and politics, unveils a tapestry woven with strategic decisions, distinctive personal characteristics, and an unparalleled adaptability that forms the bedrock of his achievements. Delving into the intricacies of Trump's journey, it becomes evident that his triumphs are not random occurrences but the result of a deliberate application of seven key pillars of strength.

Strategic Decision-Making:

Trump's career is punctuated by strategic decisions that range from brand-building to real estate investments. Each move was a calculated step, showcasing the first pillar of strength – adaptability. He understood the landscape, adjusted his strategies, and seized opportunities with precision.

Brand-Building and Real Estate Investments:

The success of Trump's brand-building efforts and real estate investments underlines the importance of determination and perseverance. His ability to weather economic downturns and navigate complex real estate landscapes illustrates the power of unwavering commitment to long-term goals.

Media Presence and Public Connection:

The pillars of courage and adaptability shine through in Trump's media presence and public connection. His courage to face scrutiny and adaptability to changing media landscapes exemplify the qualities required to not only survive but thrive in the public eye.

Populist Appeal in Politics:

The transition into politics and the appeal to populist sentiments marks the fusion of several pillars. It showcases resilience, determination, and the ability to build a supportive network, as Trump successfully connected with a diverse audience, overcoming political adversities.

Ability to Attract Success in Varied Fields:

Trump's career is a testament to the versatility inherent in the seventh pillar – the ability to attract success in various fields. His journey serves as a case study of leveraging personal strengths across diverse domains, illustrating the power of adaptability and optimism.

In essence, Donald Trump's career is not just a success story; it is a masterclass in leveraging personal strengths and seizing opportunities to achieve triumph in the face of adversities. His journey underscores the importance of resilience, determination, adaptability, courage, perseverance, optimism, and the creation of a supportive network as the pillars that can elevate an individual to unprecedented heights of success.

As readers, you now hold the keys to unlocking your potential through the wisdom embedded in these pillars. Trump's life serves as a living testament to the transformative power of embracing these principles. Apply them with purpose, and like Trump, navigate the complexities of life, turning challenges into opportunities and adversity into triumph. The journey may be demanding, but armed with these pillars, you are not just destined to succeed; you are destined to triumph in the face of any adversity. The legacy of Donald Trump's 7 pillars of strength awaits its continuation in your extraordinary journey.

As we conclude this transformative journey through 'Donald Trump's 7 Pillars of Strength,' it becomes abundantly clear that these principles are not merely words on a page but guiding lights illuminating the path to triumph in adversity. Resilience, determination, adaptability, courage, perseverance, optimism, and a supportive network are not just abstract concepts; they are the keys to unlocking unparalleled success in the face of life's challenges.

By internalizing these pillars, you are not just reading about success; you are actively participating in its creation. The strength derived from resilience will empower you to weather any storm, and determination will be the driving force propelling you toward your goals. As you embrace adaptability, you will discover the ability to navigate the unpredictable with ease, while courage becomes the armor protecting you from the doubts that may arise. Perseverance ensures that setbacks are not the end but rather stepping stones on your path to greatness. Optimism becomes a lens through which you view challenges not as obstacles but as opportunities for growth and transformation. And in building a supportive network, you forge bonds that provide strength in unity, transforming shared burdens into shared triumphs.

Since the dawn of 2015, the global spotlight has been unwaveringly fixed upon the United States of America, all thanks to the formidable presence of Donald J Trump in the realm of U.S. politics. The enigma that is the former president, Donald Trump, continues to captivate the world's attention as he embarks on a labyrinthine journey toward the upcoming November 2024 elections. As intrigue envelops us all, the burning question echoes in our minds: Can Donald J Trump, amidst a myriad of pending federal and state lawsuits, and an intricate political odyssey, emerge victorious in this impending battle? In simpler terms, will the 45th U.S. president harness the power of his 7th pillar of strength to triumph over these formidable challenges and ascend to the esteemed position of the 47th President of the United States?

Delving into the profound understanding of the potency and application of these 7th pillars of strength for triumph in adversity, I devoted considerable time to unraveling the intricacies of Donald J Trump's life, penning two comprehensive books on his captivating journey. Through personal experiences, I have witnessed the transformative power of these pillars in my own life. I am firmly convinced that Donald Trump, facing the headwinds of numerous legal battles, will ingeniously devise the next strategic move, carving uncharted paths through the formidable mountains ahead. Like an inventor crafting a shuttle to reach an unexplored planet, he will stop at nothing—even if it means metaphorically drying the ocean—to overcome the challenges in his path.

As I draw the final lines of this book, my encouragement to you reverberates with newfound vigor. Mere comprehension of these principles is not enough; true success lies in their consistent application. Their potency is universal, transcending moral and ethical boundaries. Seize control of your destiny, intricately weave these pillars into the fabric of your daily existence, and bear witness to the profound metamorphosis that unfolds before your eyes. The time for empowerment is now, and the journey toward triumph amidst adversity awaits those who dare to embrace it.

As you turn the final pages, let this not be the end, but the beginning of a new chapter in your life. Apply these principles with unwavering commitment, and in doing so, become the author of your own success story. The journey may be challenging, but armed with resilience, determination, adaptability, courage, perseverance, optimism, and a supportive network, you are not just destined to triumph; you are destined to thrive. Go forth, embrace the pillars, and let the triumph in adversity be the defining narrative of your extraordinary journey.

Contact information

Instagram: innovative genius@innovative_genius23

Twitter: innovative genius @innovativege

References:

Wonderopolis.org. (n.d.) Do you see what I see? Accessed May 19, 2020. https://wonderopolis.org/wonder/do-you-see-what-i-see.

https://www.linkedin.com/pulse/five-pillars-resilience-abstract-uk Author: David Nikolich

https://www.virtuesforlife.com/facing-challenges-the-7-pillars-of-resilience/ Author: Michael Wigge

https://sk.sagepub.com/reference/hdbk_socialpsychtheories1/n21.xml - By: Edward L. Deci and Richard M. Ryan

Olds, J., & Milner P. (1954). Positive reinforcement produced by electrical stimulation of septal area and other regions of rat brain. Journal of Comparative and Physiological Psychology, 47(6), 419–427. https://doi.org/10.1037/h0058775

https://www.merriam-webster.com/dictionary/determination

https://www.indeed.com/career-advice/career-development/determination

https://www.theforage.com/blog/skills/adaptability - By: Zoe Kaplan

https://hbr.org/2011/07/adaptability-the-new-competitive-advantagev - By: Martin Reeves and Mike Deimler

https://www.betterup.com/blog/adaptability - by Allaya Cooks - Campbell

https://enhancv.com/resume-skills/flexibility/ - By: Volen Vulkov

https://www.dictionary.com/browse/adaptability

https://www.authentichappiness.sas.upenn.edu/newsletters/authentichappinesscoaching/courage

https://en.wikipedia.org/wiki/Courage

https://link.springer.com/referenceworkentry/10.1007/978-3-319-28099-8_498-1

https://www.merriam-webster.com/dictionary/courage

https://positivepsychology.com/perseverance/ - By: Anna Katharina Schaffner, Ph.D.

https://www.commonsensemedia.org/articles/what-is-perseverance

https://dictionary.cambridge.org/us/dictionary/english/persevere

Gardner, C. (2009). Start where you are: Life lessons in getting from where you are to where you want to be. HarperCollins Publishers

Lyubomirsky, S. (2008). The how of happiness: A new approach to getting the life you want. Penguin Group.

Harris, R. (2008). The happiness trap: How to stop struggling and start living: A guide to ACT. Trumpeter Books.

Peltz, L. (2013).The mindful path to addiction recovery: A practical guide to regaining control over your life. Shambhala Publications.

https://www.sciencedirect.com/science/article/pii/S1319157823004366

https://trumpwhitehouse.archives.gov/briefings-statements/letter-president-donald-j-trump-emergency-determination-stafford-act/

https://trumpwhitehouse.archives.gov/briefings-statements/letter-president-donald-j-trump-emergency-determination-stafford-act/

Supreme Court says Trump can appear on 2024 ballot, overturning Colorado ruling - cbsnews

The 3 Objective Ways to Determine Donald Trump's Success obsesrver.com

Achen CH, Bartels LM (2016) Democracy for Realists: Why Elections Do Not Produce Responsive Government. Princeton, NJ: Princeton University Press.

Aiolfi T (2022) Populism as a transgressive style. Global Studies Quarterly 2(1): 1–12.

Allern S, Pollack E (eds) (2012) Scandalous! The Mediated Construction of Political Scandals in Four Nordic Countries. Gothenburg: Nordicom.

Begley P, Bochel C, Bochel H, et al. (2019) Assessing policy success and failure: targets, aims and processes. Policy Studies 40(2): 188–204.

Bovens MAP, Hart P (1998) Understanding Policy Fiascoes. Piscataway, NJ: Transaction Publishers

Brandt SL (2020) Donald Trump, the reality show: populism as performance and spectacle. Zeitschrift für Literaturwissenschaft und Linguistik 50(2): 303–321.

Butler J (2016) Trump is emancipating unbridled hatred. Zeit Online, 26 October. https://www.zeit.de/kultur/2016-10/jucith-butler-donald-trump-populism-interview/seite-2

Canovan M (1999) Trust the people! Populism and the two faces of democracy. Political Studies 47: 2–16.

Casullo ME (2020b) The body speaks before it even talks: deliberation, populism and bodily representation. Journal of Deliberative Democracy 16(1): 27–36.

Cha T (2016) The return of Jacksonianism: the international implications of the Trump phenomenon. The Washington Quarterly 39(4): 83–97.

Donovan T, Redlawsk D (2018) Donald Trump and right-wing populists in comparative perspective. Journal of Elections, Public Opinion and Parties 28(2): 190–207.

Ferguson T, Page BI, Rothschild J, et al. (2020) The roots of right-wing populism: Donald Trump in 2016. International Journal of Political Economy 49(2): 102–123.

James TS (ed.) (2022) The Trump Administration: The President's Legacy within and beyond America. New York: Routledge.

Lawrence RG, Boydstun AE (2017) What we should really be asking about media attention to Trump. Political Communication 34(1): 150–153.

Ostiguy P, Roberts KM (2016) Putting Trump in comparative perspective: populism and the politicization of the socio-cultural low. Brown Journal of World Affairs 23: 25–50.

Shanahan M (2019) Outsider presidents: comparing Trump and Eisenhower. In: Oliva M, Shanahan M (eds) The Trump Presidency: From Campaign Trail to World Stage. Berlin: Springer, pp.9–32.